HAUNTED HISTORY

T0011676

PHANTOM SOLDIER

by **Leah Kaminski**

Illustrations by Candy Briones

BEARPORT
PUBLISHING

Minneapolis, Minnesota

BEAR CLAW

Credits

22T, ©Los Angeles/Wikimedia; 22B, ©sivarock/Getty Images

DISCLAIMER: This graphic story is a dramatization based on true events. It is intended to give the reader a sense of the narrative rather than a presentation of actual details as they occurred.

Library of Congress Cataloging-in-Publication Data

Names: Kaminski, Leah, author. | Briones, Candy, 1987- illustrator.
Title: Phantom soldier / by Leah Kaminski ; illustrations by Candy Briones.
Description: Bear claw. | Minneapolis, Minnesota : Bearport Publishing, [2020] | Series: Haunted history | Includes bibliographical references and index.
Identifiers: LCCN 2020008700 (print) | LCCN 2020008701 (ebook) | ISBN 9781647470111 (library binding) | ISBN 9781647470180 (paperback) | ISBN 9781647470258 (ebook)
Subjects: LCSH: Ghosts–England–Derby–Juvenile literature. | Ghosts–England–Derby–Comic books, strips, etc. | Graphic novels. | Graphic novels.
Classification: LCC BF1472.E53 K36 2020 (print) | LCC BF1472.E53 (ebook) | DDC 133.109425/17–dc23
LC record available at https://lccn.loc.gov/2020008700
LC ebook record available at https://lccn.loc.gov/2020008701

For more information, write to Bearport Publishing, 5357 Penn Avenue South, Minneapolis, MN 55419.
Printed in the United States of America.

CONTENTS

HAUNTED HOSPITALS

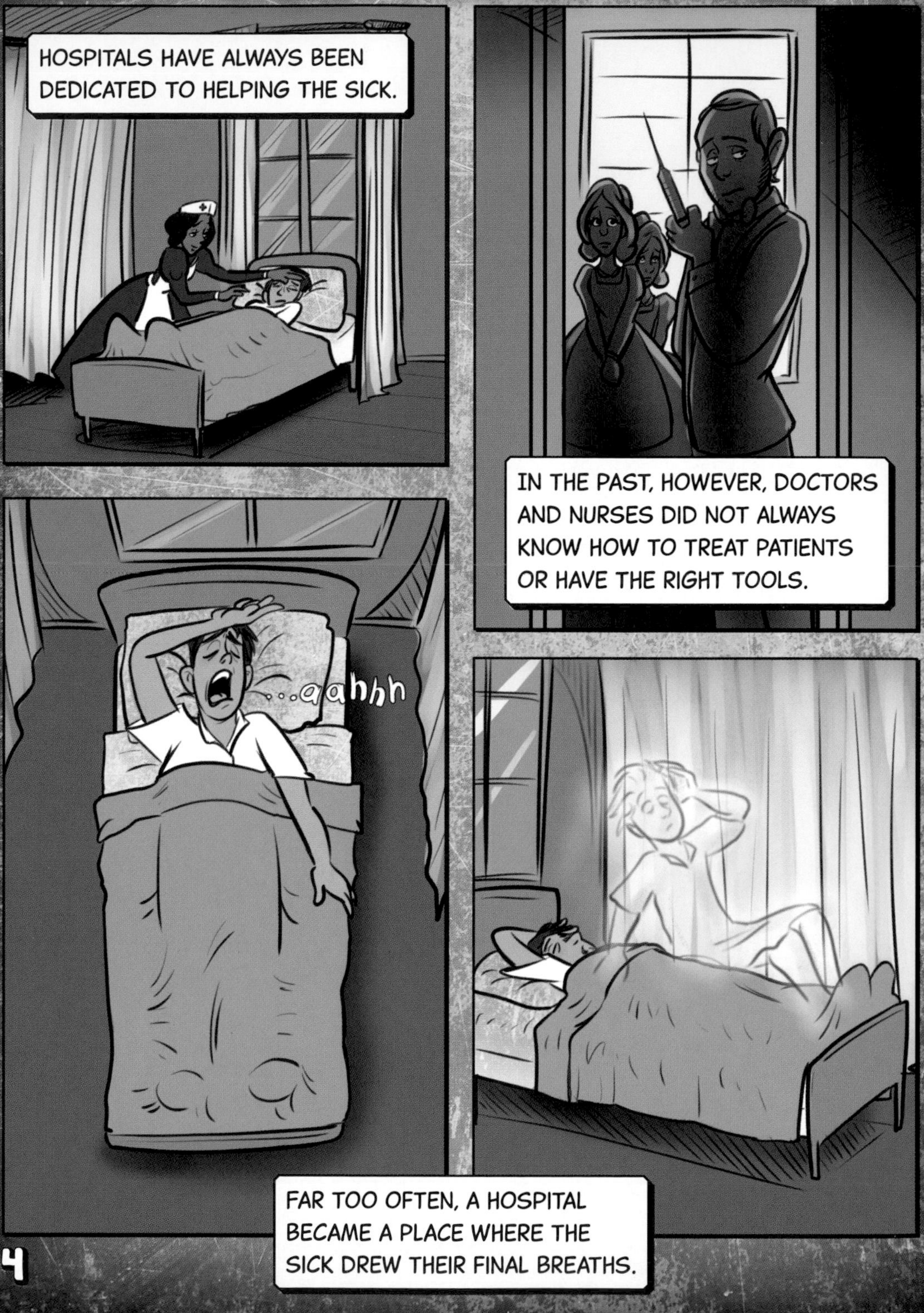
HOSPITALS HAVE ALWAYS BEEN DEDICATED TO HELPING THE SICK.
IN THE PAST, HOWEVER, DOCTORS AND NURSES DID NOT ALWAYS KNOW HOW TO TREAT PATIENTS OR HAVE THE RIGHT TOOLS.
...aahhh
FAR TOO OFTEN, A HOSPITAL BECAME A PLACE WHERE THE SICK DREW THEIR FINAL BREATHS.

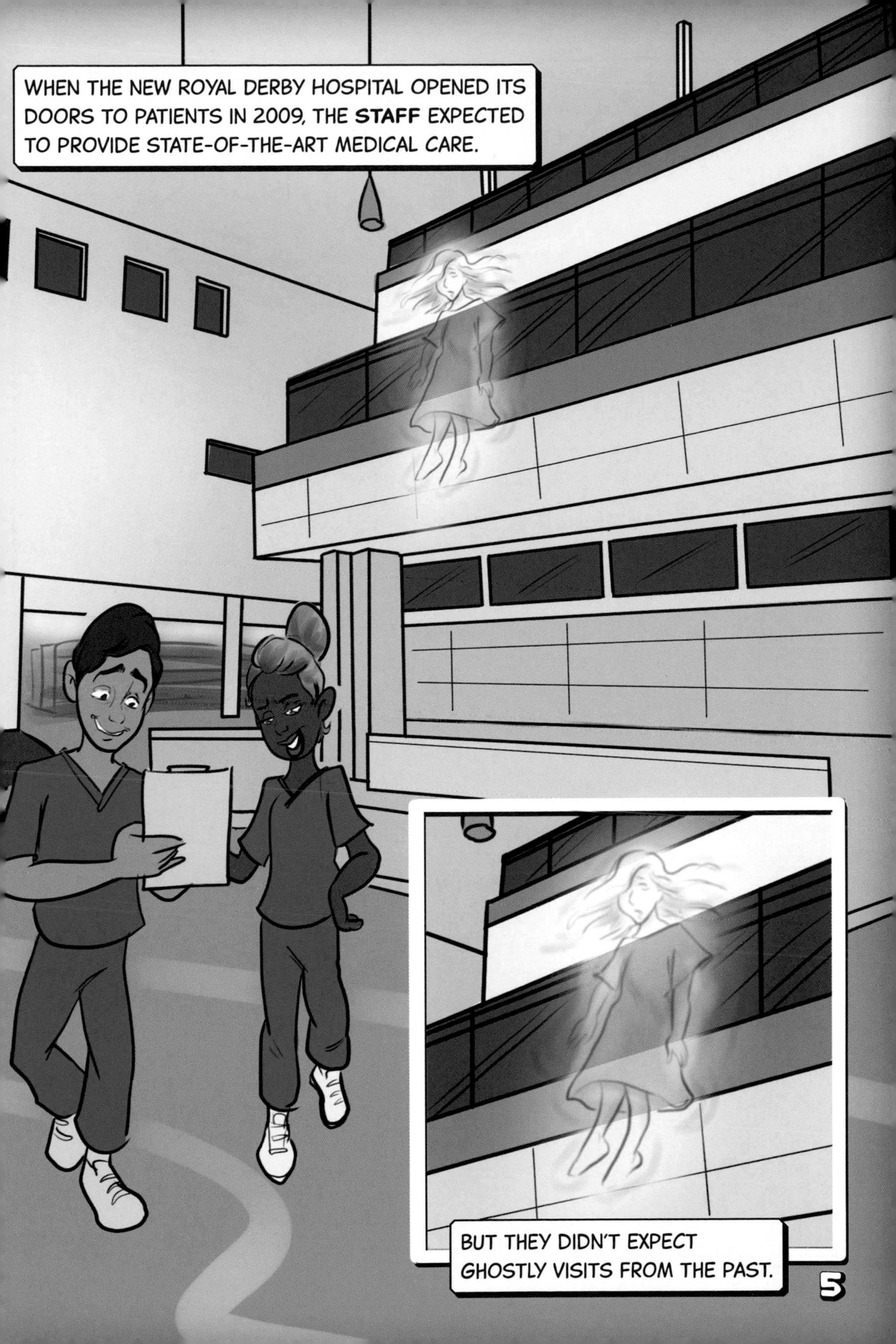
WHEN THE NEW ROYAL DERBY HOSPITAL OPENED ITS DOORS TO PATIENTS IN 2009, THE **STAFF** EXPECTED TO PROVIDE STATE-OF-THE-ART MEDICAL CARE.
BUT THEY DIDN'T EXPECT GHOSTLY VISITS FROM THE PAST.

THE GHOST CAPITAL

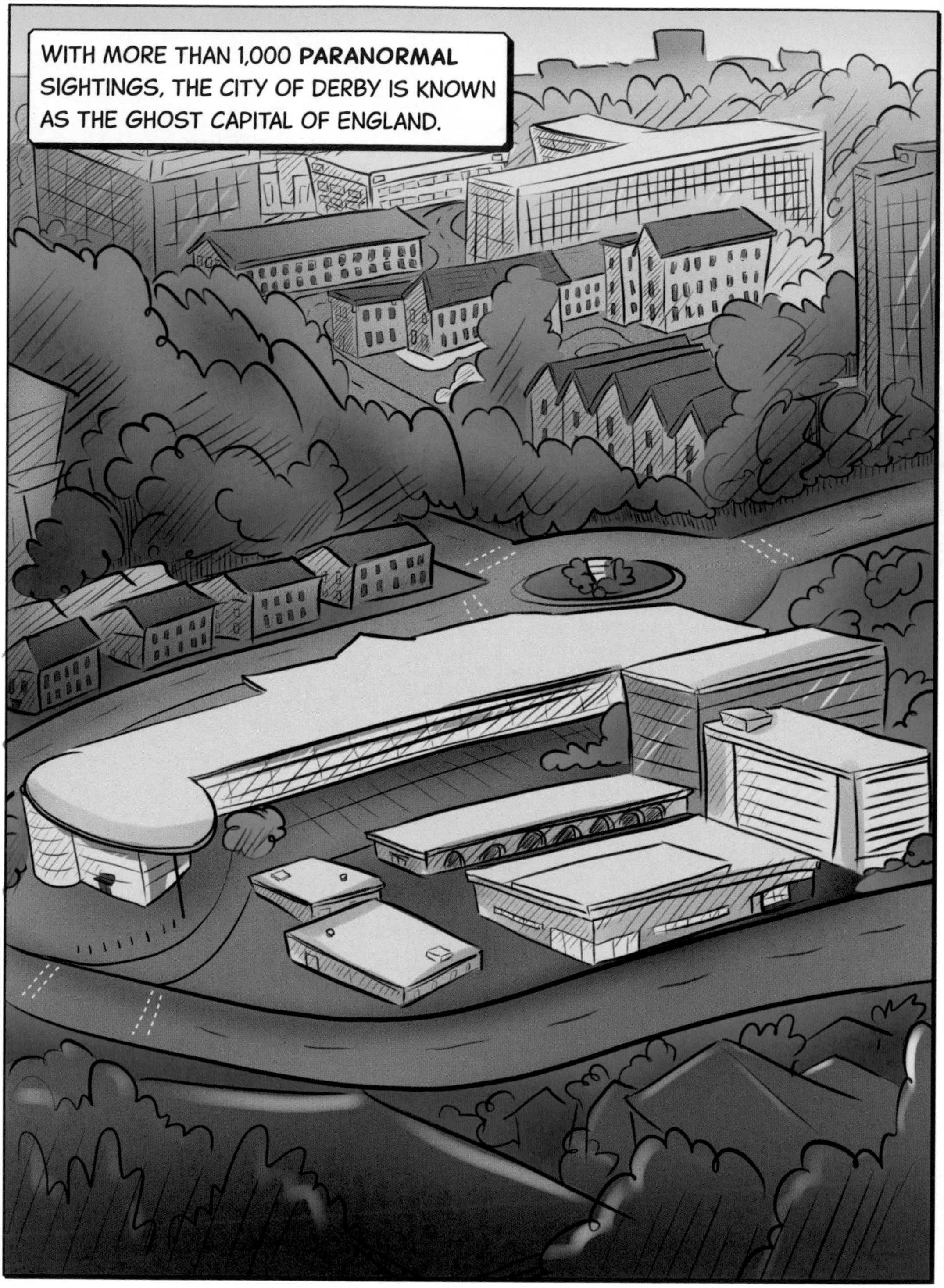
WITH MORE THAN 1,000 **PARANORMAL** SIGHTINGS, THE CITY OF DERBY IS KNOWN AS THE GHOST CAPITAL OF ENGLAND.

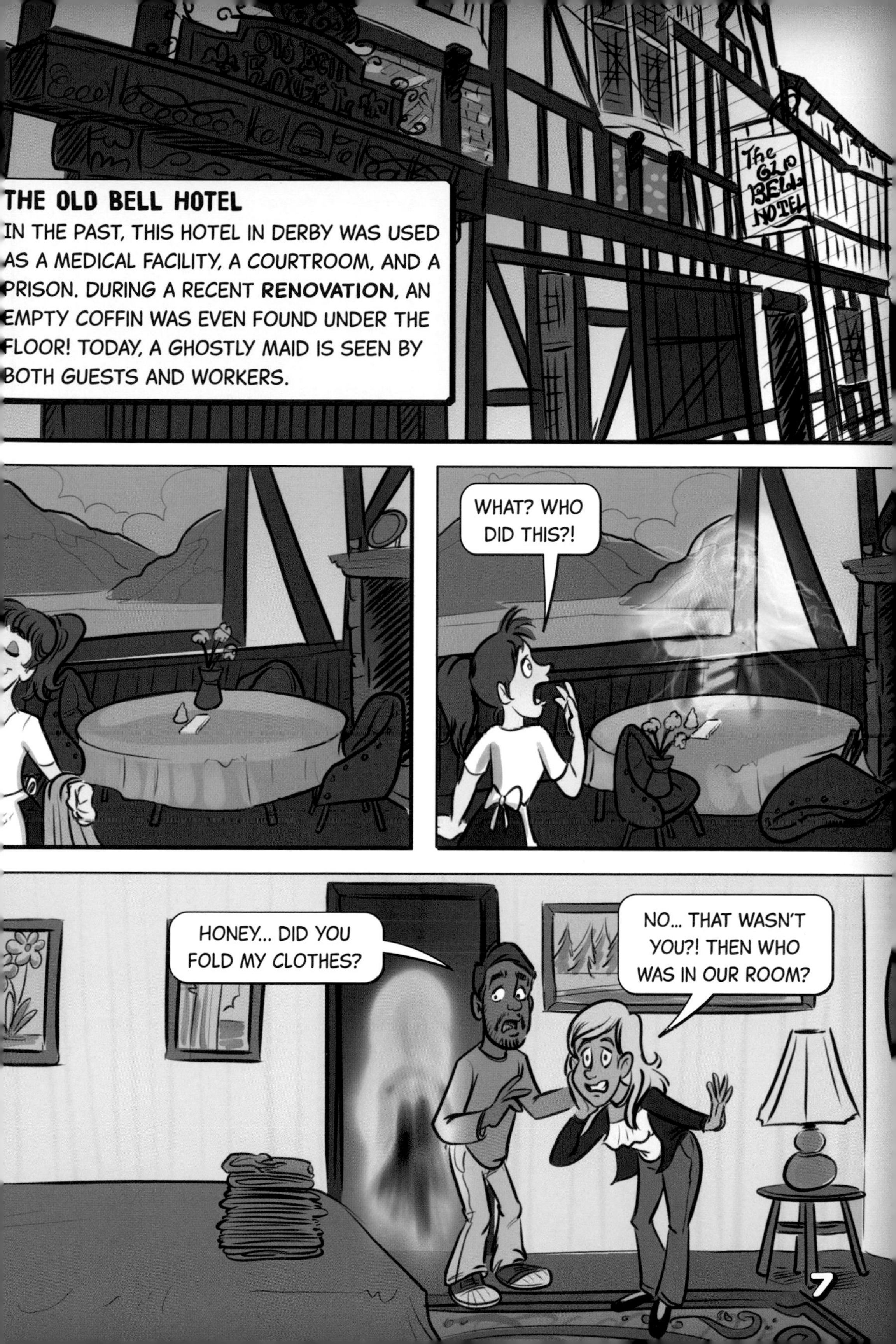
THE OLD BELL HOTEL
IN THE PAST, THIS HOTEL IN DERBY WAS USED AS A MEDICAL FACILITY, A COURTROOM, AND A PRISON. DURING A RECENT **RENOVATION**, AN EMPTY COFFIN WAS EVEN FOUND UNDER THE FLOOR! TODAY, A GHOSTLY MAID IS SEEN BY BOTH GUESTS AND WORKERS.
WHAT? WHO DID THIS?!
HONEY... DID YOU FOLD MY CLOTHES?
NO... THAT WASN'T YOU?! THEN WHO WAS IN OUR ROOM?

JAIL OF DERBY

IN THE PAST, HUNDREDS OF CRIMINALS WERE HANGED AT THE **GALLOWS** IN DERBY. TODAY, THIS JAIL IS A MUSEUM. VISITORS CAN SEE CELLS THAT ONCE HELD PRISONERS. BUT SOMETIMES, THEY FIND THAT THE CELLS ARE NOT QUITE EMPTY....

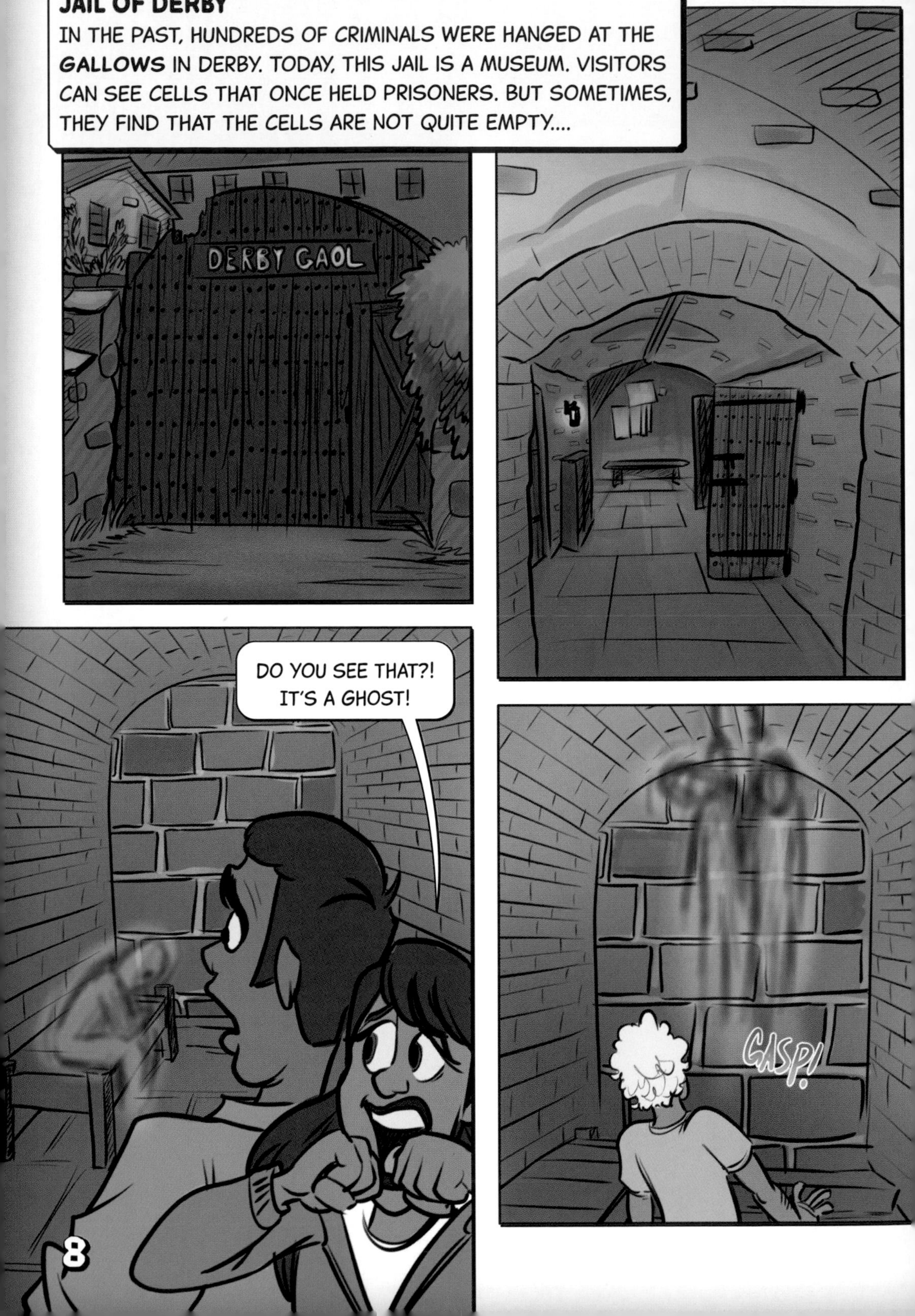
DERBY GAOL
DO YOU SEE THAT?! IT'S A GHOST!
GASP!

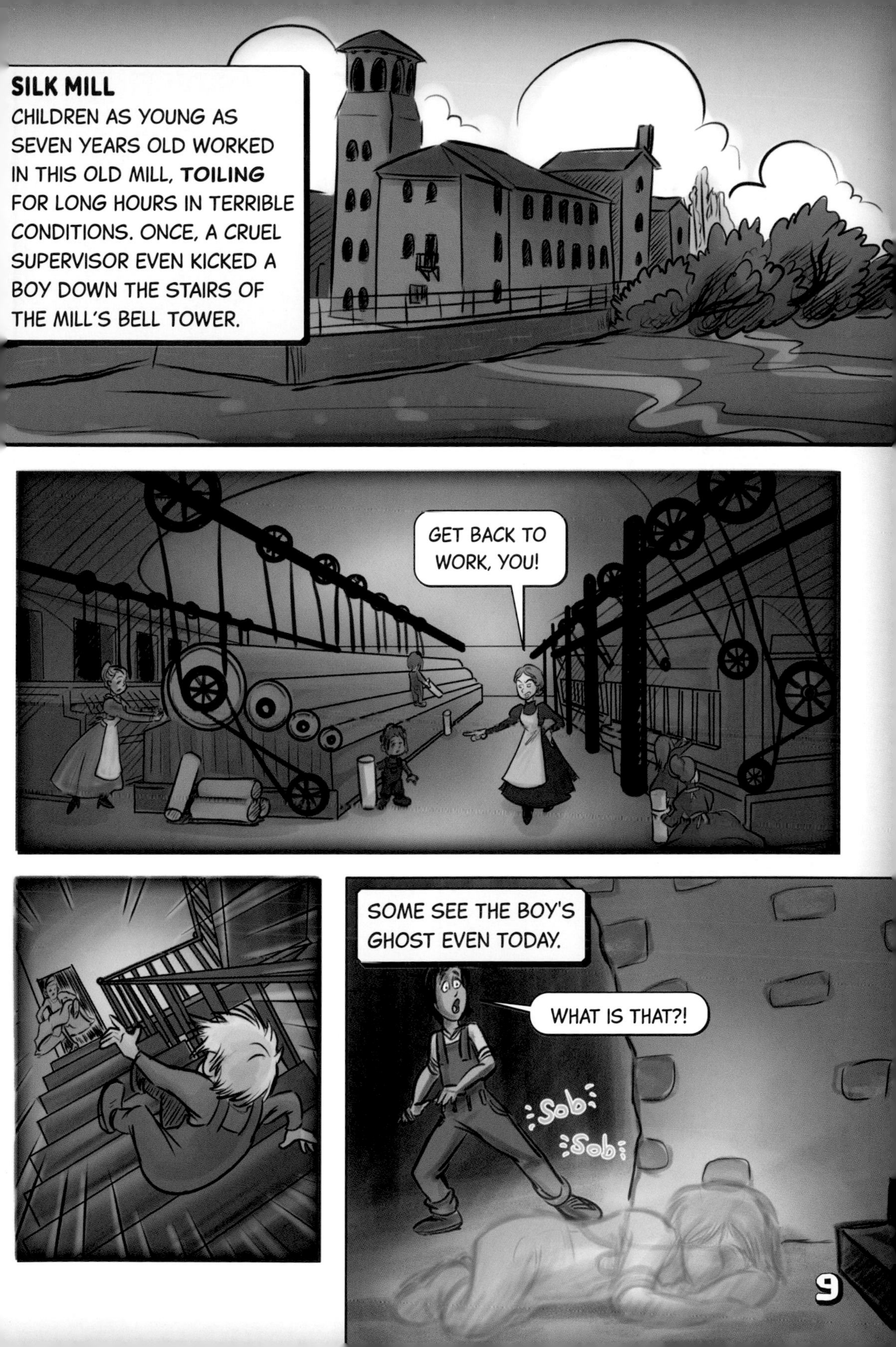
SILK MILL
CHILDREN AS YOUNG AS SEVEN YEARS OLD WORKED IN THIS OLD MILL, TOILING FOR LONG HOURS IN TERRIBLE CONDITIONS. ONCE, A CRUEL SUPERVISOR EVEN KICKED A BOY DOWN THE STAIRS OF THE MILL'S BELL TOWER.
GET BACK TO WORK, YOU!
SOME SEE THE BOY'S GHOST EVEN TODAY.
WHAT IS THAT?!
SOB
SOB

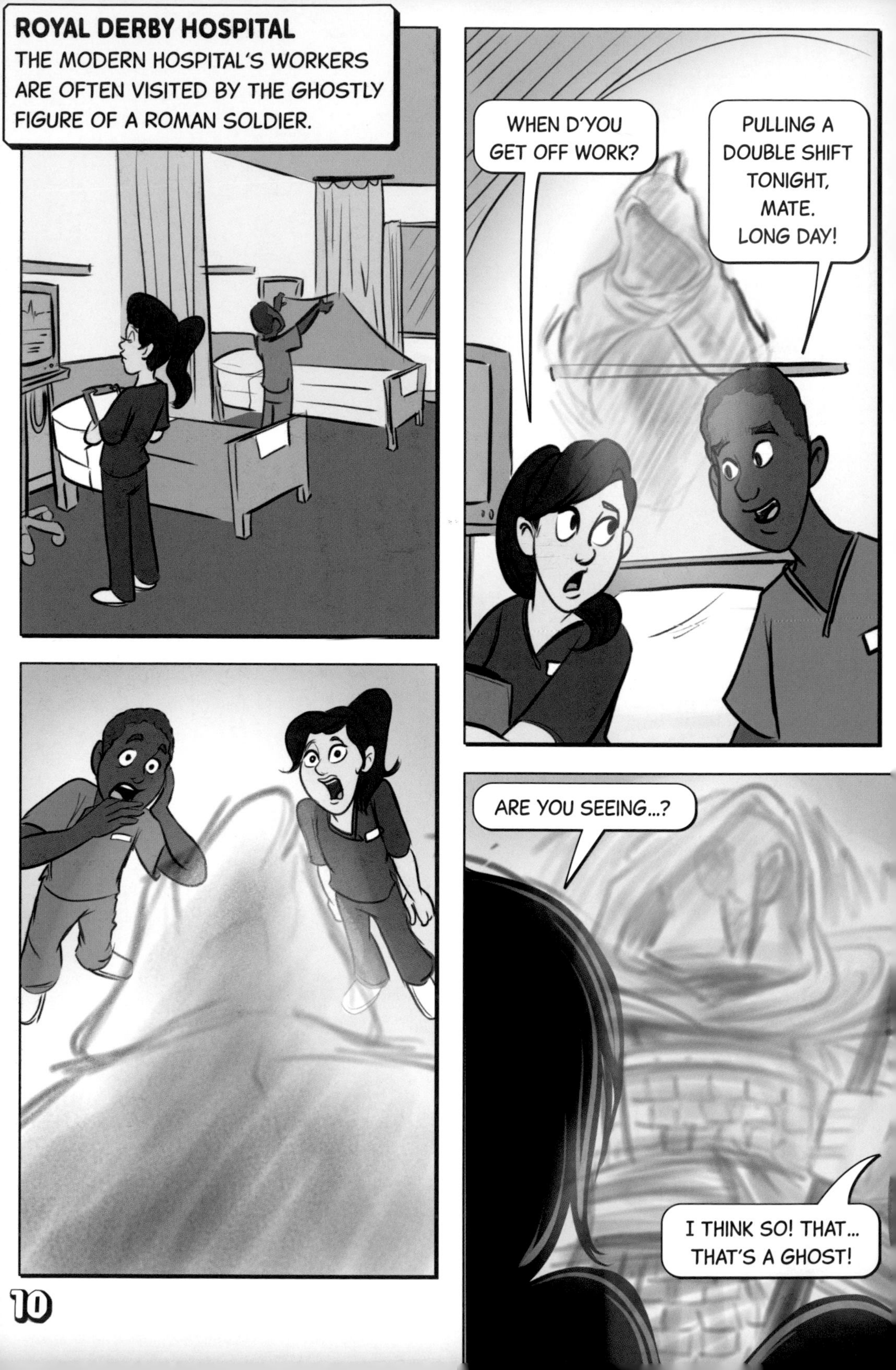
ROYAL DERBY HOSPITAL
THE MODERN HOSPITAL'S WORKERS ARE OFTEN VISITED BY THE GHOSTLY FIGURE OF A ROMAN SOLDIER.
WHEN D'YOU GET OFF WORK?
PULLING A DOUBLE SHIFT TONIGHT, MATE. LONG DAY!
ARE YOU SEEING...?
I THINK SO! THAT... THAT'S A GHOST!

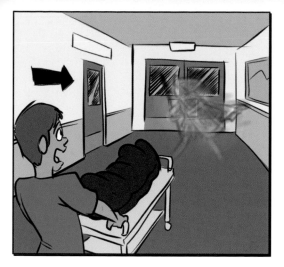

WHO—WHAT...? SOMEONE HELP!

IT WAS THERE! RIGHT THERE!

WORKERS HAVE SEEN THE **PHANTOM** SOLDIER WALK THROUGH WALLS. HE SUDDENLY APPEARS AND THEN QUICKLY DISAPPEARS. WHY WOULD A GHOST HAUNT A BRAND-NEW HOSPITAL?

DISTURBING A ROMAN ROAD

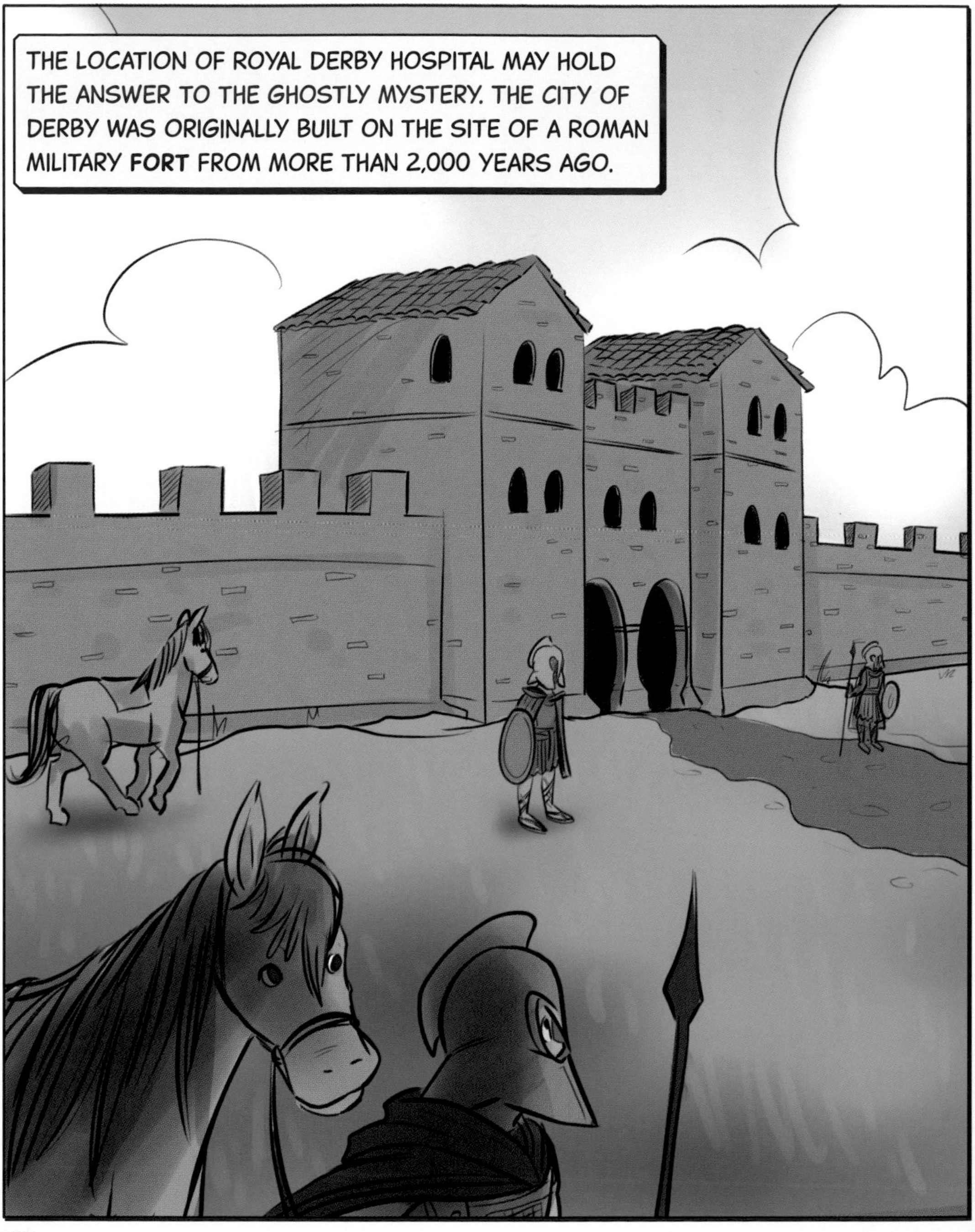
THE LOCATION OF ROYAL DERBY HOSPITAL MAY HOLD THE ANSWER TO THE GHOSTLY MYSTERY. THE CITY OF DERBY WAS ORIGINALLY BUILT ON THE SITE OF A ROMAN MILITARY **FORT** FROM MORE THAN 2,000 YEARS AGO.

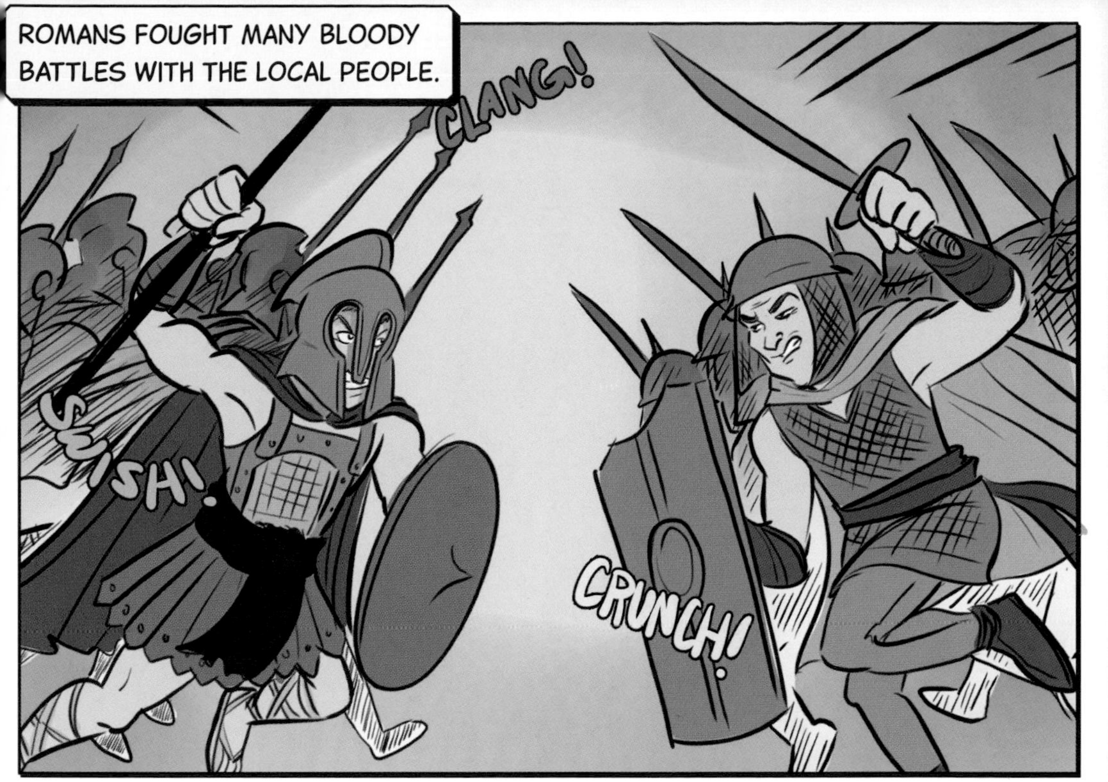
ROMANS FOUGHT MANY BLOODY BATTLES WITH THE LOCAL PEOPLE.
CLANG!
SWISH!
CRUNCH!

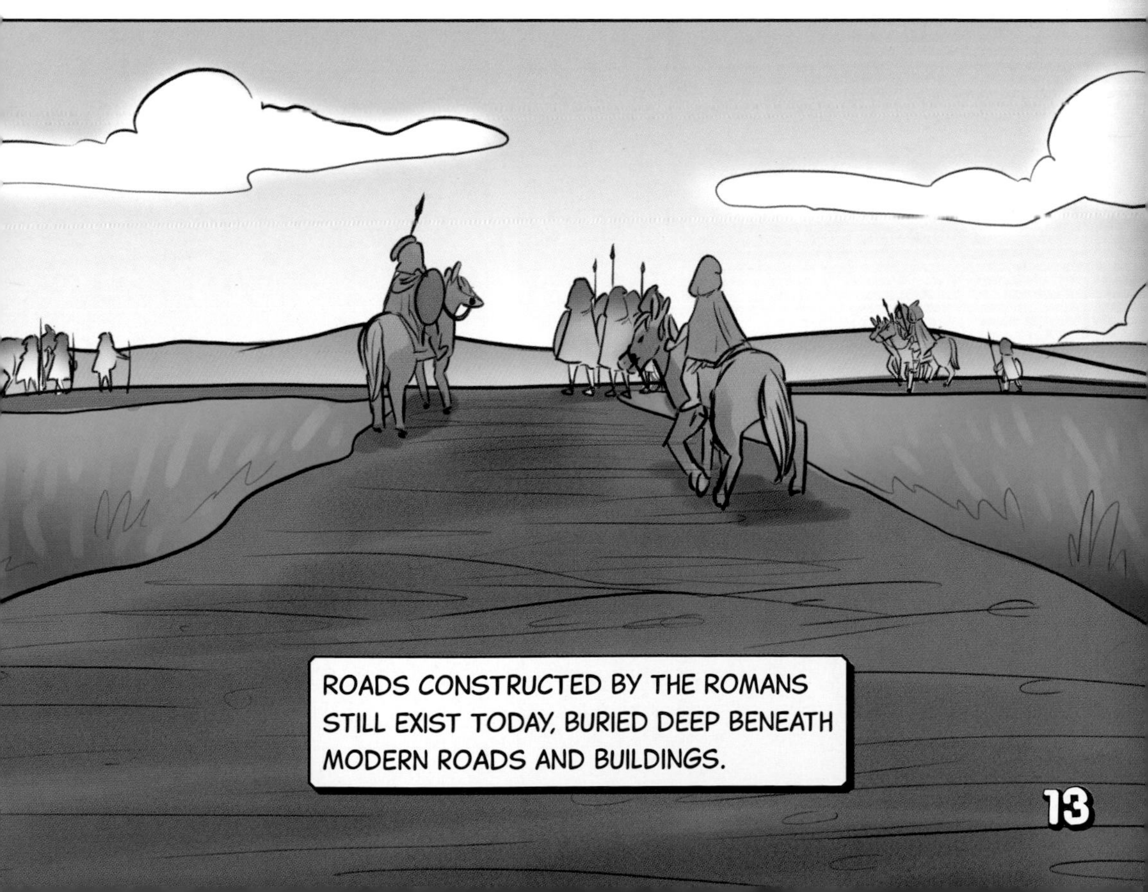
ROADS CONSTRUCTED BY THE ROMANS STILL EXIST TODAY, BURIED DEEP BENEATH MODERN ROADS AND BUILDINGS.

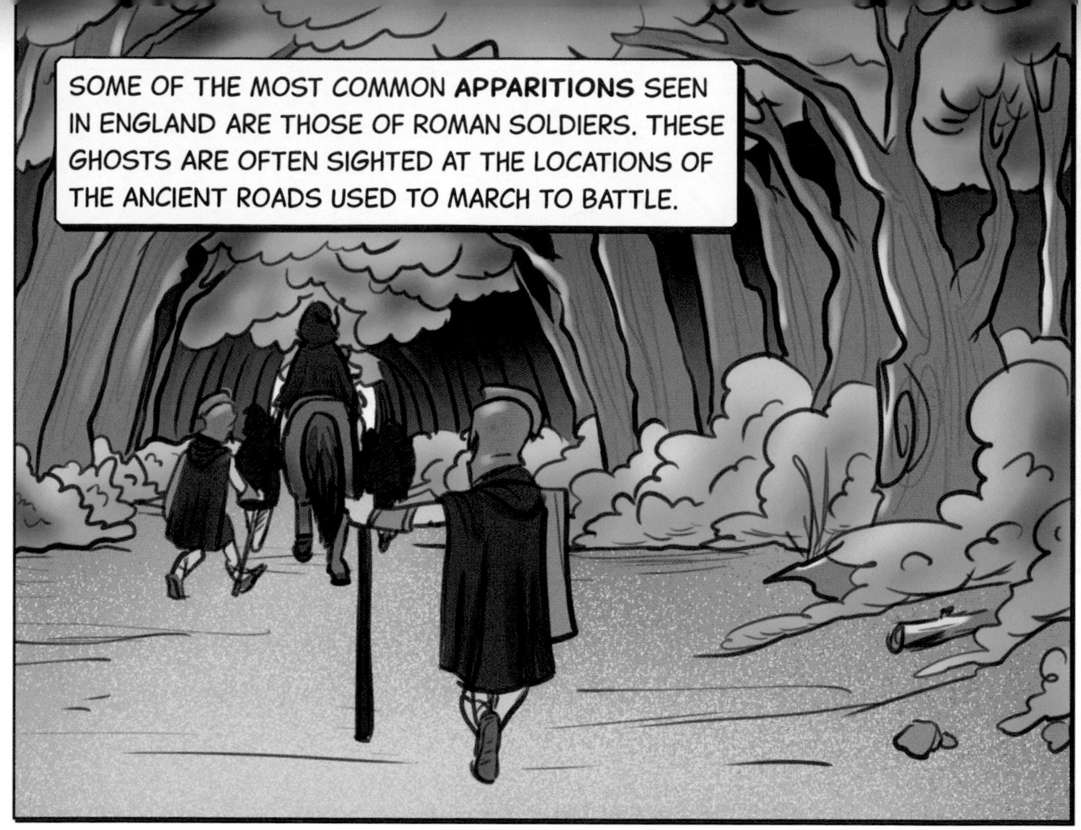
SOME OF THE MOST COMMON APPARITIONS SEEN IN ENGLAND ARE THOSE OF ROMAN SOLDIERS. THESE GHOSTS ARE OFTEN SIGHTED AT THE LOCATIONS OF THE ANCIENT ROADS USED TO MARCH TO BATTLE.

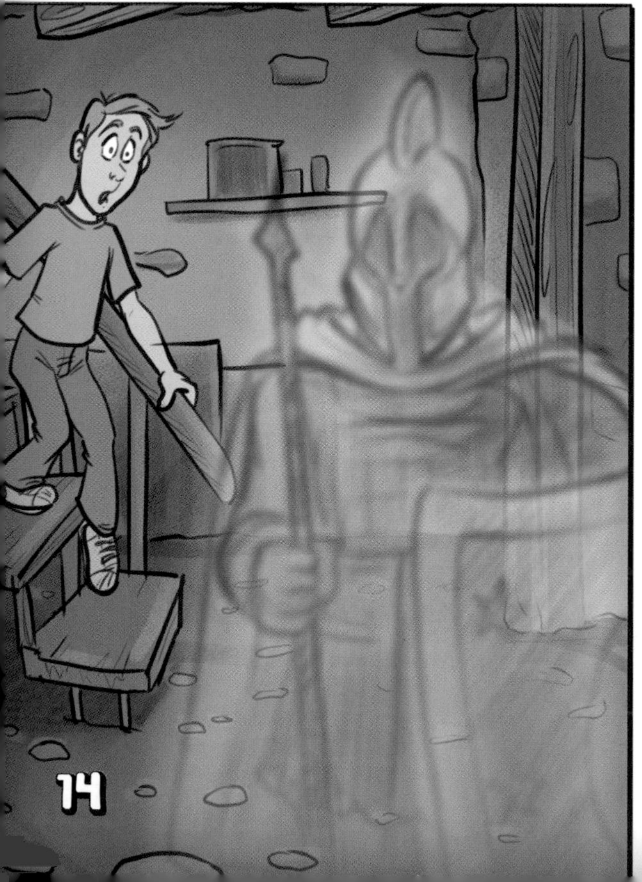

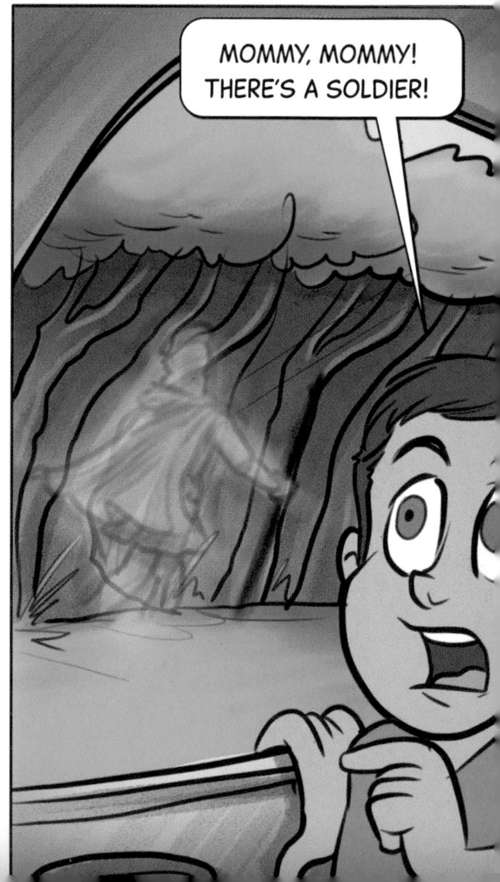
MOMMY, MOMMY!
THERE'S A SOLDIER!

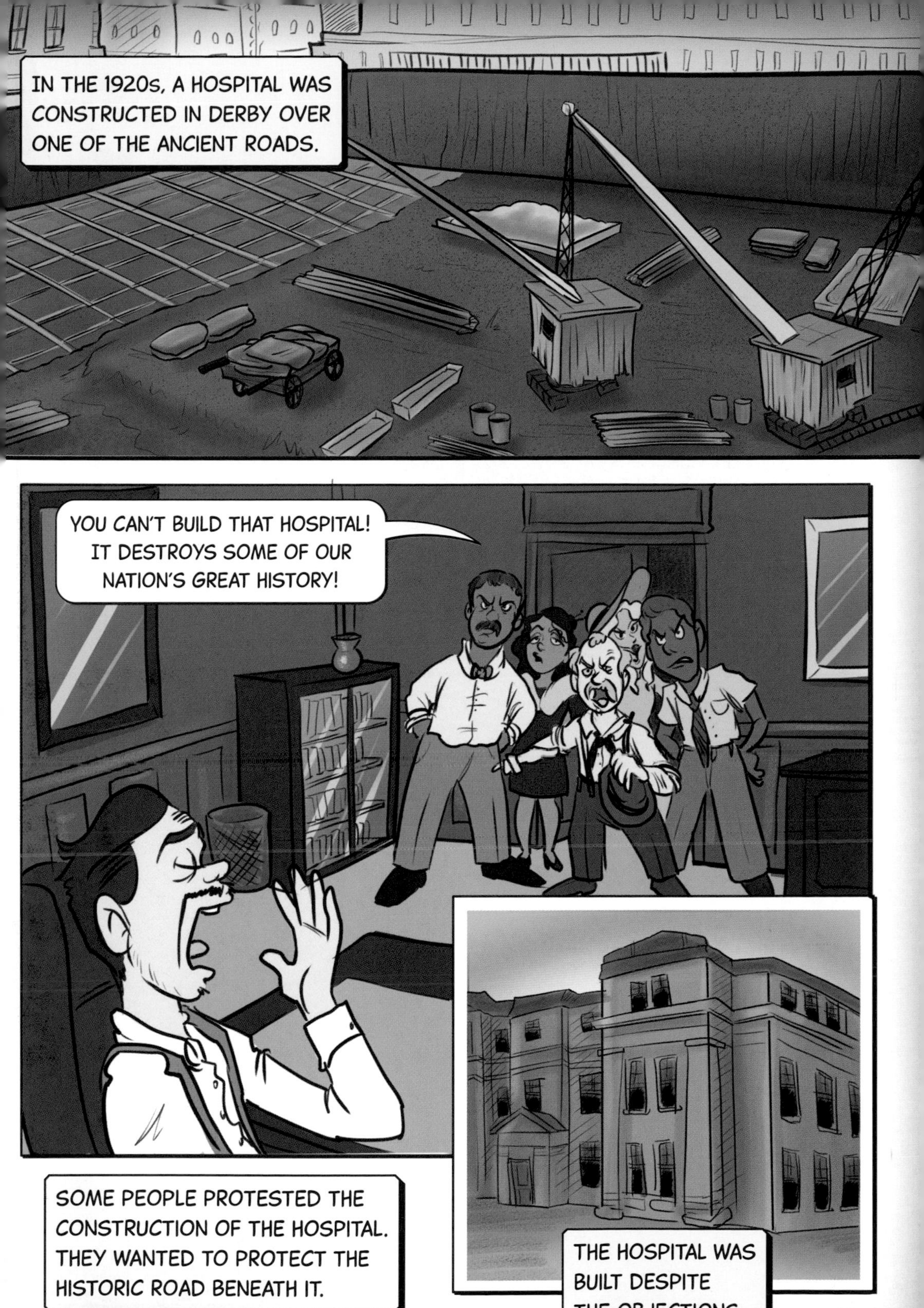
IN THE 1920s, A HOSPITAL WAS CONSTRUCTED IN DERBY OVER ONE OF THE ANCIENT ROADS.
YOU CAN'T BUILD THAT HOSPITAL! IT DESTROYS SOME OF OUR NATION'S GREAT HISTORY!
SOME PEOPLE PROTESTED THE CONSTRUCTION OF THE HOSPITAL. THEY WANTED TO PROTECT THE HISTORIC ROAD BENEATH IT.
THE HOSPITAL WAS BUILT DESPITE THE OBJECTIONS.

GHOST SOLDIER

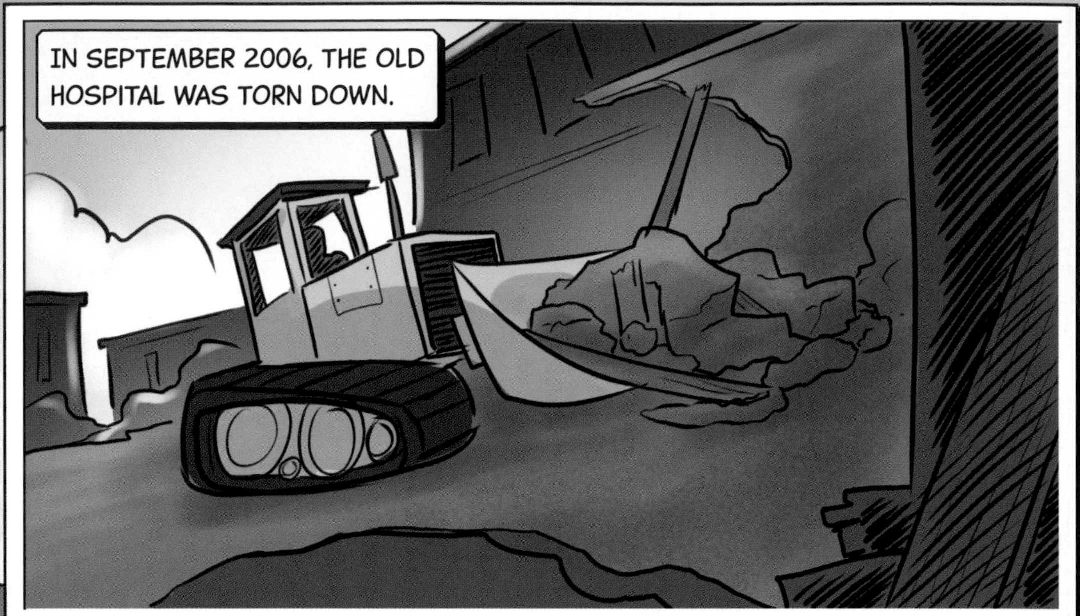
IN SEPTEMBER 2006, THE OLD HOSPITAL WAS TORN DOWN.

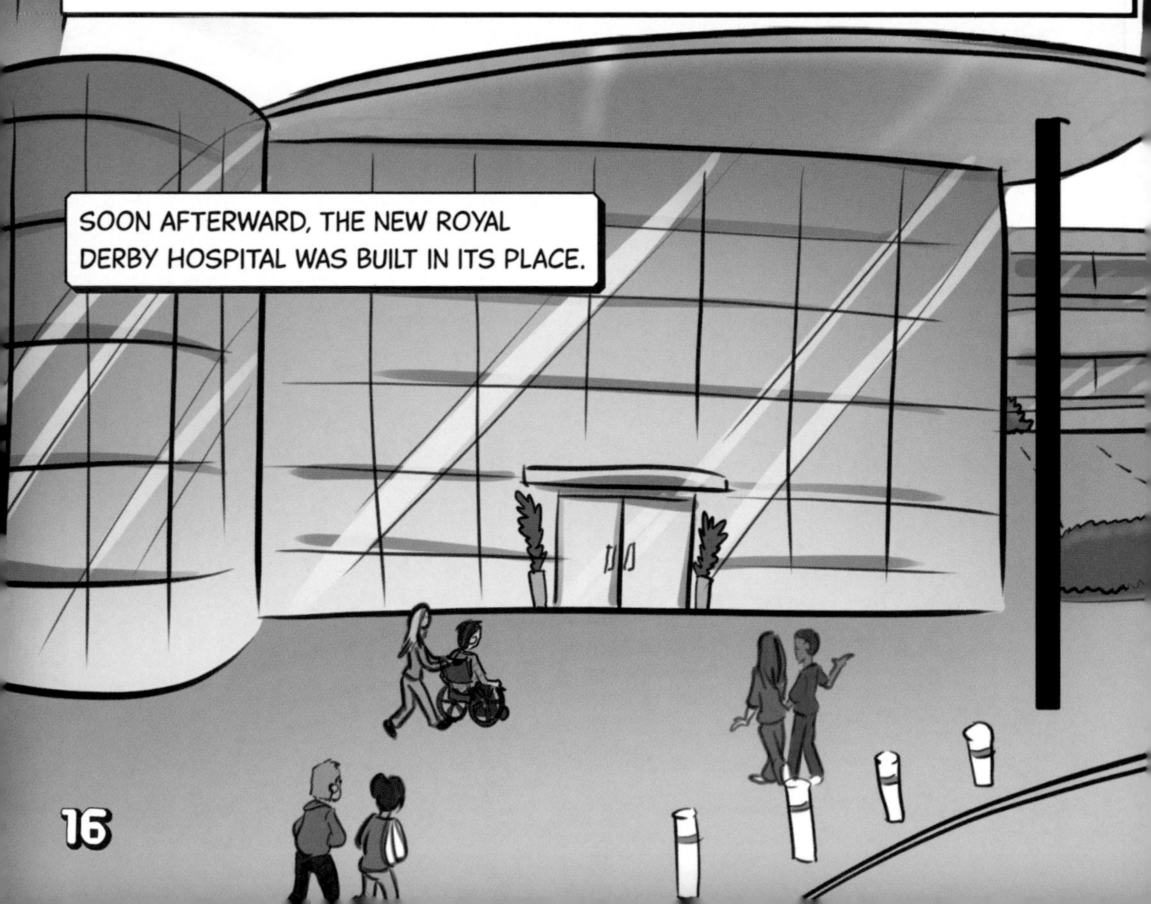
SOON AFTERWARD, THE NEW ROYAL DERBY HOSPITAL WAS BUILT IN ITS PLACE.

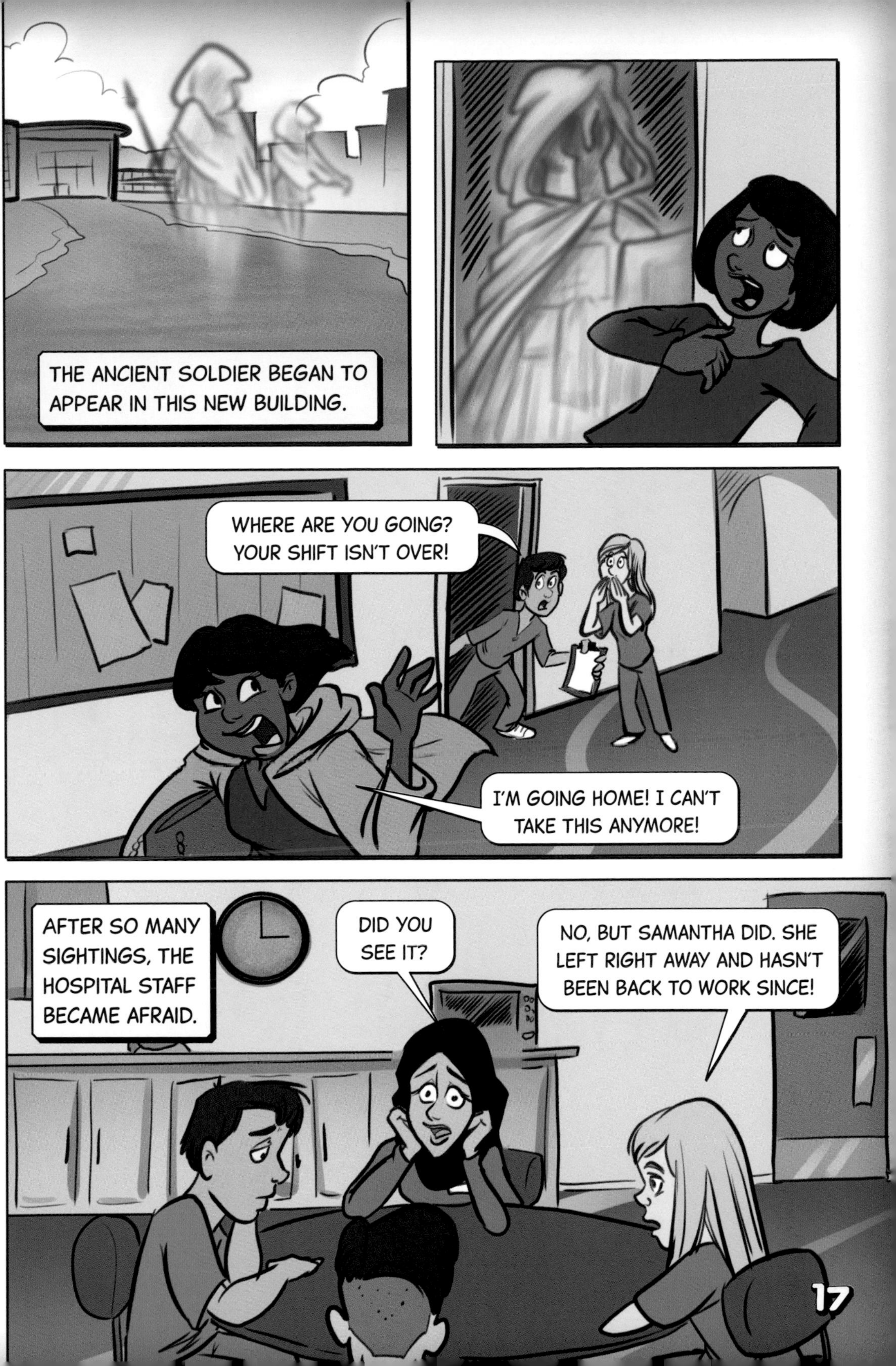
THE ANCIENT SOLDIER BEGAN TO APPEAR IN THIS NEW BUILDING.
WHERE ARE YOU GOING? YOUR SHIFT ISN'T OVER!
I'M GOING HOME! I CAN'T TAKE THIS ANYMORE!
AFTER SO MANY SIGHTINGS, THE HOSPITAL STAFF BECAME AFRAID.
DID YOU SEE IT?
NO, BUT SAMANTHA DID. SHE LEFT RIGHT AWAY AND HASN'T BEEN BACK TO WORK SINCE!

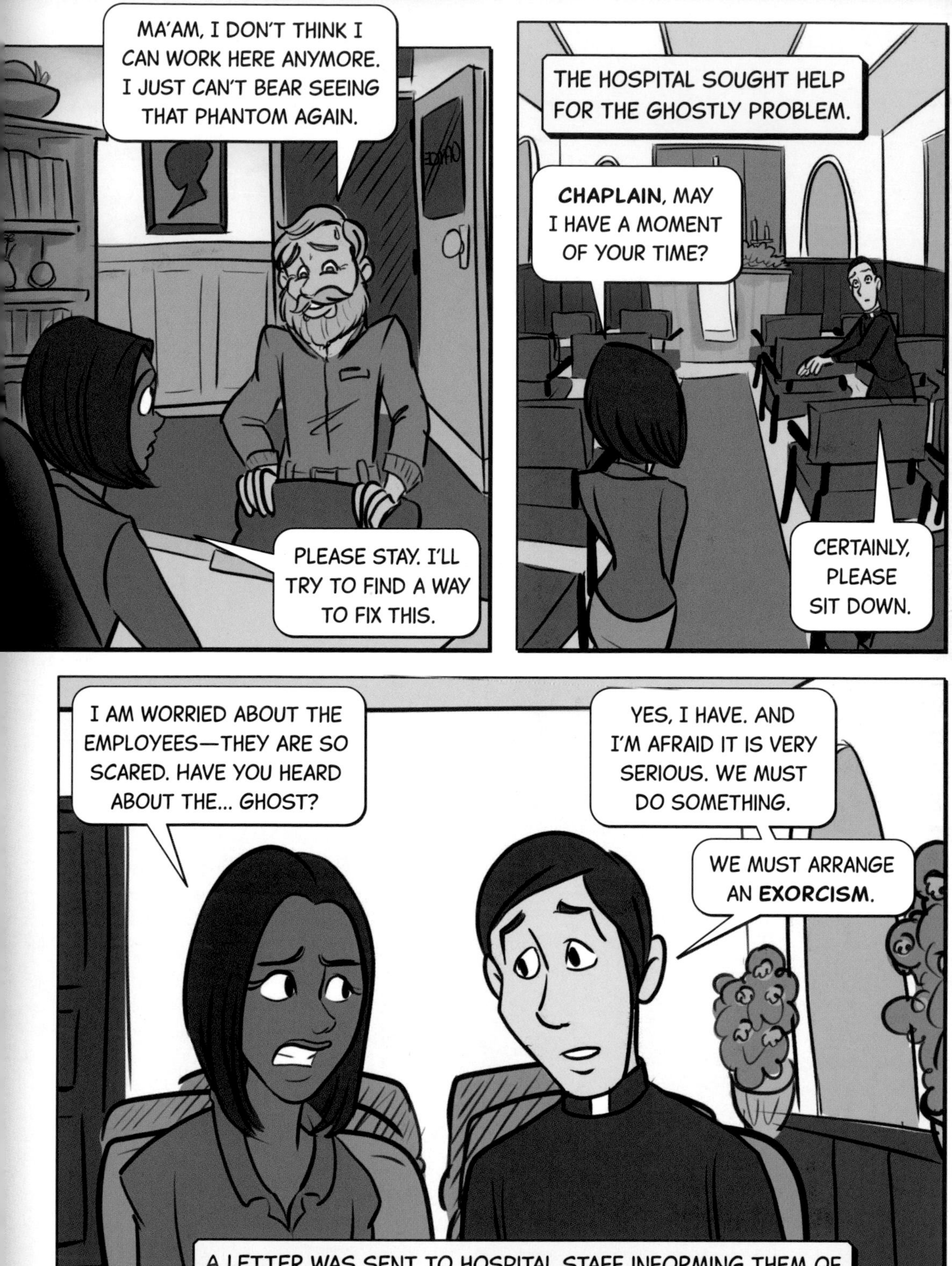
MA'AM, I DON'T THINK I CAN WORK HERE ANYMORE. I JUST CAN'T BEAR SEEING THAT PHANTOM AGAIN.
PLEASE STAY. I'LL TRY TO FIND A WAY TO FIX THIS.
THE HOSPITAL SOUGHT HELP FOR THE GHOSTLY PROBLEM.
CHAPLAIN, MAY I HAVE A MOMENT OF YOUR TIME?
CERTAINLY, PLEASE SIT DOWN.
I AM WORRIED ABOUT THE EMPLOYEES—THEY ARE SO SCARED. HAVE YOU HEARD ABOUT THE... GHOST?
YES, I HAVE. AND I'M AFRAID IT IS VERY SERIOUS. WE MUST DO SOMETHING.
WE MUST ARRANGE AN **EXORCISM**.
A LETTER WAS SENT TO HOSPITAL STAFF INFORMING THEM OF A PLANNED EXORCISM. BUT AFTER THE PUBLIC HEARD ABOUT THE PLAN, THE HOSPITAL DECIDED TO CANCEL THE EXORCISM.

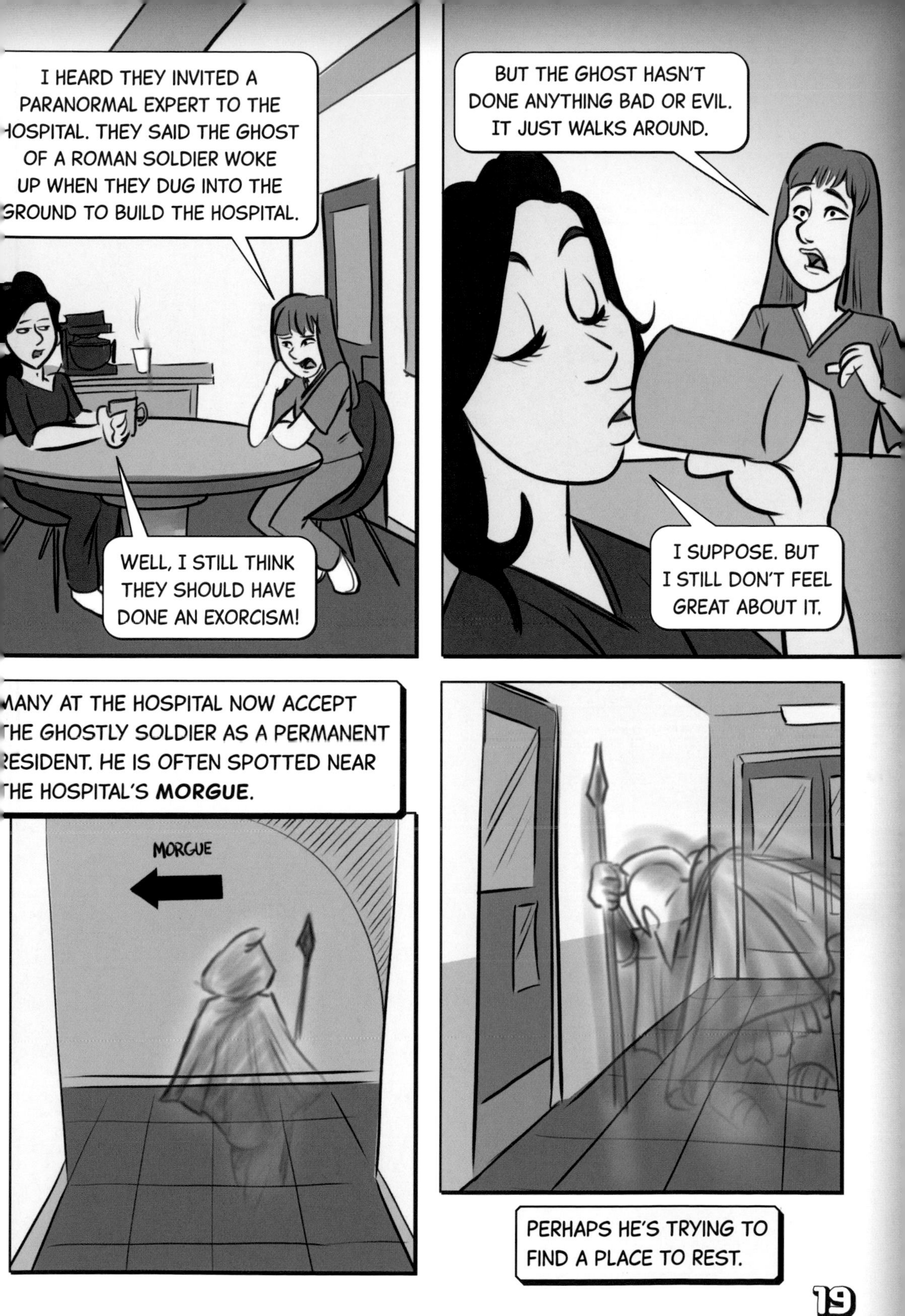
I HEARD THEY INVITED A PARANORMAL EXPERT TO THE HOSPITAL. THEY SAID THE GHOST OF A ROMAN SOLDIER WOKE UP WHEN THEY DUG INTO THE GROUND TO BUILD THE HOSPITAL.
WELL, I STILL THINK THEY SHOULD HAVE DONE AN EXORCISM!
BUT THE GHOST HASN'T DONE ANYTHING BAD OR EVIL. IT JUST WALKS AROUND.
I SUPPOSE. BUT I STILL DON'T FEEL GREAT ABOUT IT.
MANY AT THE HOSPITAL NOW ACCEPT THE GHOSTLY SOLDIER AS A PERMANENT RESIDENT. HE IS OFTEN SPOTTED NEAR THE HOSPITAL'S **MORGUE**.
MORGUE
PERHAPS HE'S TRYING TO FIND A PLACE TO REST.

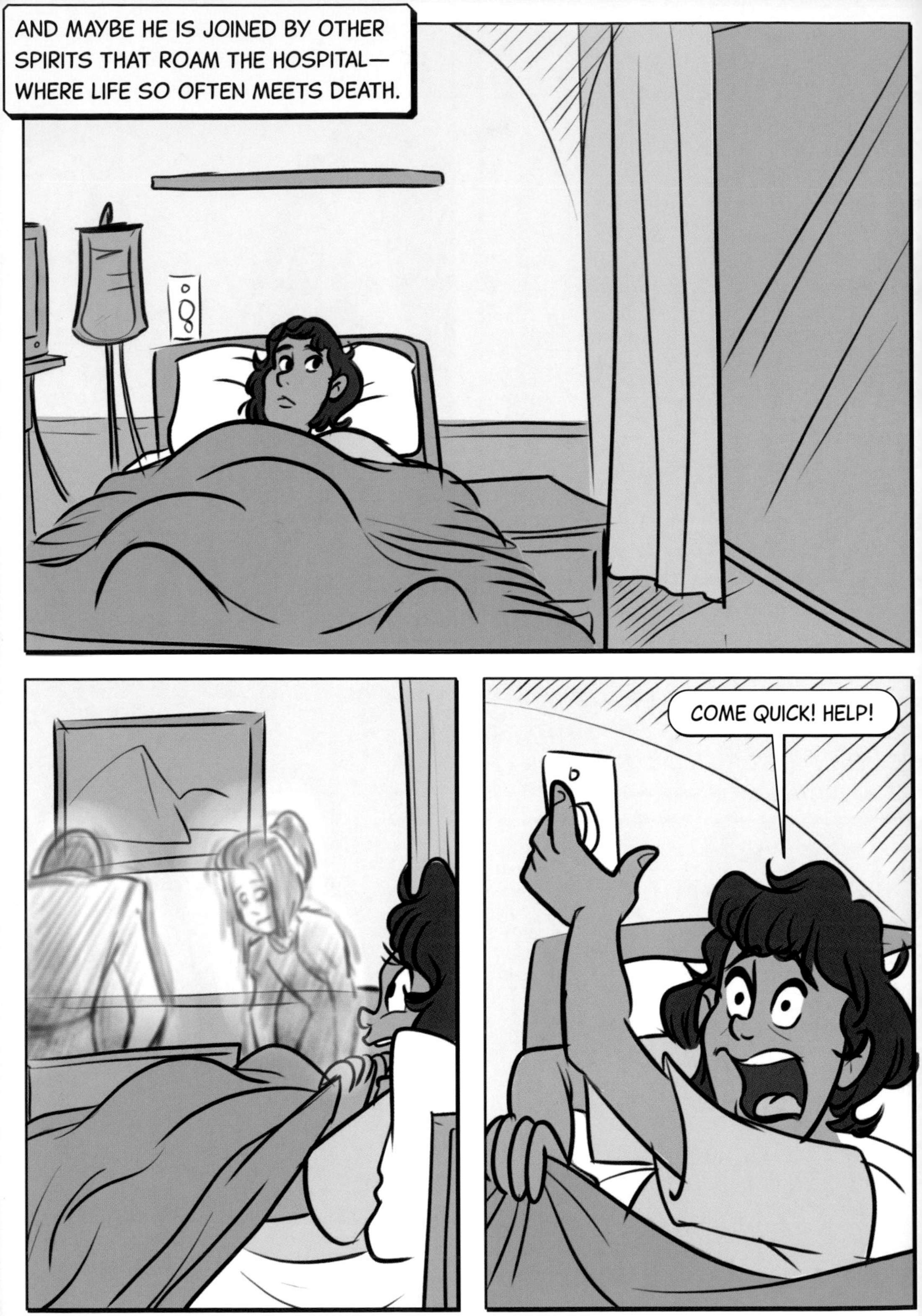
AND MAYBE HE IS JOINED BY OTHER SPIRITS THAT ROAM THE HOSPITAL— WHERE LIFE SO OFTEN MEETS DEATH.
COME QUICK! HELP!

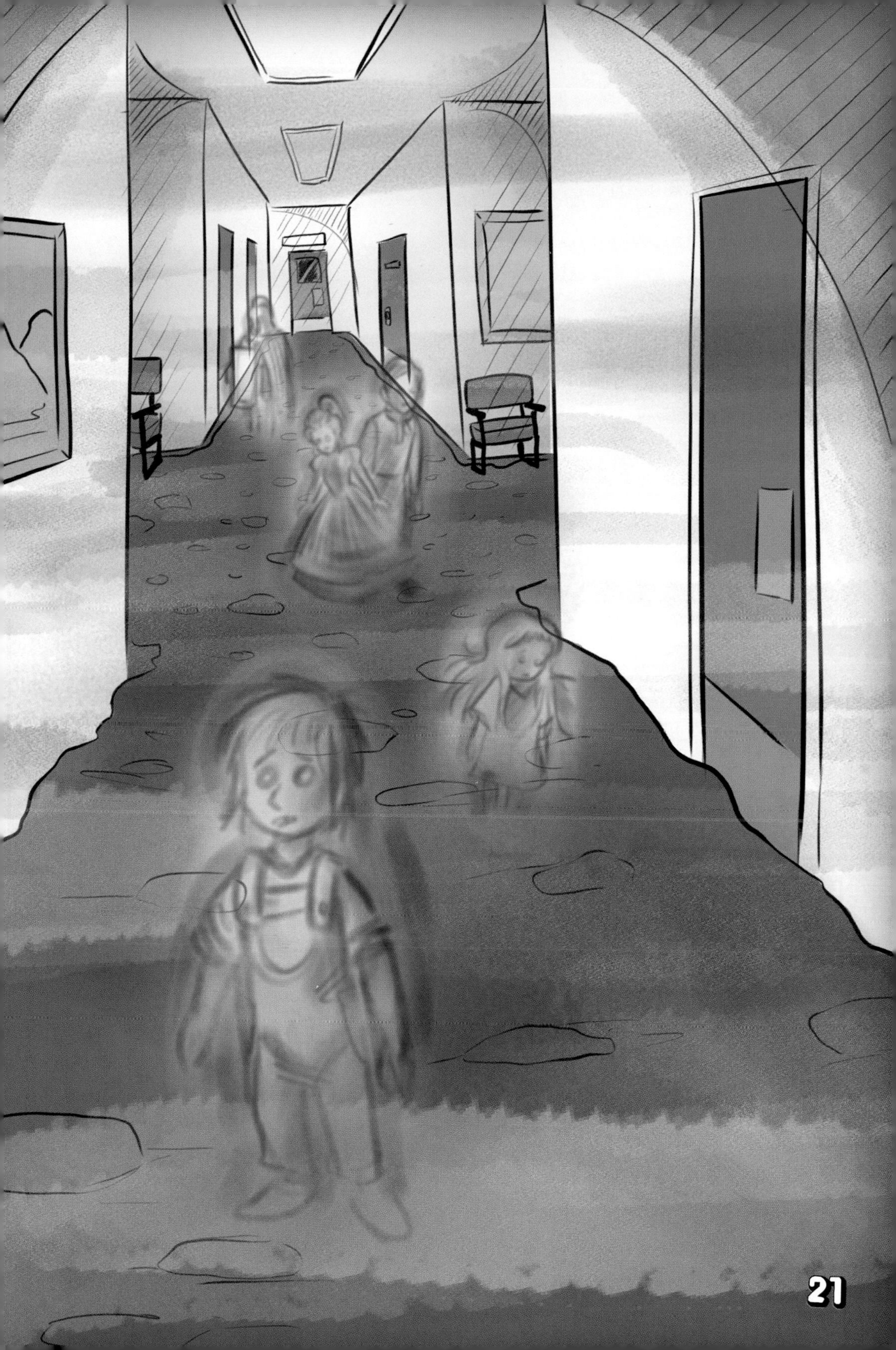

OTHER HAUNTED
HOSPITALS

LINDA VISTA HOSPITAL
LOS ANGELES, CALIFORNIA

Linda Vista Hospital in Los Angeles was built in 1904. At first, the hospital was known for its excellent care. After closing in 1991, the building became known for its ghosts! Some people have heard a girl crying on the fifth floor. Others have seen a ghostly doctor or a strange green light at night. The empty hospital has even been used as the setting for several horror movies!

OLD CHANGI HOSPITAL
CHANGI, SINGAPORE

During World War II (1939–1945), the Japanese invaded Singapore. For three years, they were very cruel to Singapore's citizens. A hospital in Changi was used as a prison by the Japanese secret police. They hurt prisoners to try to get information from them. In 1997, the Old Changi Hospital was shut down. Today, ghosts of the victims are sometimes spotted at the abandoned hospital. They're often seen missing their heads and feet!

GLOSSARY

apparitions ghosts or ghostlike images

chaplain a priest or religious leader associated with a non-religious institution, such as a school, prison, or hospital

exorcism the act of forcing a ghost or spirit to leave a place

fort a strong building that is used during battles for protection

gallows a wooden frame used to hang criminals

morgue a place where dead bodies are kept before being buried

paranormal events that are not able to be scientifically explained

phantom a ghost or spirit

renovation the process of fixing or improving a building

staff people who work for a business

toiling working extremely hard

INDEX

READ MORE

Andrus, Aubre, Megan Cooley Peterson, and Ebony Joy Wilkins. *Real-Life Ghost Stories: Spine-Tingling True Tales.* North Mankato, MN: Capstone Press (2020).

Markovics, Joyce. *Deadly Morgues (Tiptoe into Scary Places).* New York: Bearport Publishing (2018).

Wood, Alix. *Abandoned Hospitals (World's Scariest Places).* New York: Gareth Stevens Publishing (2017).

LEARN MORE ONLINE

1. Go to **www.factsurfer.com**

2. Enter "**Phantom Soldier**" into the search box.

3. Click on the cover of this book to see a list of websites.